Medicinal Mushrooms

for Immune Enhancement:

Agaricus Blazei Murill

DISCOVER THE BETA GLUCAN SECRET!

A Health Learning Handbook

Beth M. Ley, Ph.D.

BL Publications
Detroit Lakes, MN

BL Publications, Detroit Lakes, MN
email: blpub@tekstar.com
www.blpbooks.com
For orders call 1-877-BOOKS11

Library of Congress Cataloging-in-Publication Data

Ley, Beth M., 1964-
Medicinal mushrooms for immune enhancement : agaricus blazei murill, discover the beta glucan secret! / Beth M. Ley.--
p. cm.
Includes bibliographical references and index.
ISBN 1-890766-15-1
1. Agaricus--Therapeutic use--Popular works.
2. Immunological adjuvants--Popular works. 3. Antineoplastic agents--Popular works. 4. Anticholesteremic agents--Popular works. I. Title.
RM666.M87 L49 2001
615'.3296--dc21

00-012992

Printed in the United States of America

This book is not intended as medical advice. Its purpose is solely educational. Please consult your healthcare professional for all health problems.

Credits

Cover Design: BL Publications
Technical Assistance: Craig Hewitt
Proofreading: Deborah Brenk

YOU NEED TO KNOW...
THE HEALTH MESSAGE

Do you not know that you are God's temple and that God's Spirit dwells in you? If anyone destroys God's temple, God will destroy him, For God's temple is holy and that temple you are.
1 Corinthians 3:16-17

So, whether you eat or drink, or whatever you do, do all to the glory of God.
1 Corinthians 10:31

Table of Contents

Introduction

There is a lot more to mushrooms than good taste! Mushrooms have been used throughout Asia for thousands of years for their health-promoting properties.

Mushrooms belong to the fungi family. Most of you know that not all mushrooms are health-promoting. Some are indeed highly toxic, others are hallucinogenic, and not all are good tasting – some are quite bitter. This book will concentrate on the health-promoting aspects of mushrooms, and specifically, the species Agaricus Blazei Murill.

The edible mushrooms are a valuable health food as they are low in calories, high in vegetable proteins, chitin, iron, zinc, fiber, essential amino acids, and other vitamins and minerals.

Mushrooms have a long history of use in Traditional Chinese Medicine. Their legendary effects on promoting good health and vitality and increasing your body's adaptive abilities have been supported by recent scientific studies. These studies suggest that mushrooms help our body strengthen itself and fight off illness by maintaining physiological homeostasis - restoring our bodies balance and enhancing our natural resistance to disease.

Mushrooms contain a variety of compounds which can have powerful immune system enhancement properties. Several different polysaccharide anti-tumor agents

> ***Use your food as your medicine***
> ***and your medicine as your food.***
> **Hippocrates**

have been developed from various medicinal mushrooms. Both cellular components and secondary metabolites of a large number of mushrooms have been shown to benefit our immune system and therefore could be used to prevent and treat a variety of health problems. They are currently used as adjuncts to cancer treatments in Japan and China and are also used throughout the world including the United States to promote the immune system and benefit a variety of health problems.

The Immune System

The basic function of the immune system is to protect us against infection, illness and disease of all kinds. It fights off thousands of predatory environmental and infectious microorganisms which can invade and damage virtually every part of the body. The immune system expels pathogens, toxic chemicals and tumorous cells generated through mutation. The immune system also aids the body in tissue repair and healing. It's goal is to maintain homeostasis (balance) in the body.

The immune system involves a finely-tuned, highly-integrated cascade of events that destroy a would-be invader. Once the immune system identifies an unwanted guest, it brings an awesome array of chemical and cellular weapons to act towards its elimination. This non-specific, intricate and elaborate immune response with built-in checks and balances can readily discriminate between the "self" and "non-self," that is, the invading pathogens. The intricate network of the immune response ensures that the body does not turn on itself and lose the ability to distinguish between self and non-self.

Autoimmunity

Loss of the ability to distinguish between self and non-self can lead to autoimmunity, and the body may manufacture antibodies and T-cells directed against its own cells, cell components or specific organs. Autoimmune conditions include allergies, asthma, rheumatoid arthritis, dermatitis, diabetes, Systemic Lupus Erythematosus, Multiple Sclerosis, fibromyalgia and also may underlie numerous additional chronic diseases. Overstimulation caused by constant exposure to various pathogens, may also result in autoimmunity.

Weakened Immunity

When the immune system is working properly, we remain healthy. However, the immune system can and does become compromised. This may be a result of constant environmental assault (such as from exposure to pseudo-estrogens, pesticides and pollutants in air, food and water, certain medications and various other toxins), persistent metabolic damage (for example, high free radical stress), poor nutrition, chronic infection or advancing age. Strenuous physical activity and emotional stress are also known to adversely affect immunity. Numerous diverse factors may compromise the immune system and disturb its various components exquisitely balanced.

It is no secret that our immune systems are under huge amounts of stress today. This excess stress weakens the immune system making us more vulnerable to illness. When our bodies become overwhelmed, the regulatory features of the immune system weaken and become less effective resulting in:

- Fatigue, loss of stamina and energy
- Frequent colds and infections
- Loss of appetite and weight loss
- Fever, night sweats
- Skin rashes and cold sores
- Diarrhea
- Increased severity in allergy symptoms
- Swollen lymph nodes, etc.

In time, this can result in a more serious immunocompromised condition (such as chronic fatigue, cancer, HIV, etc.). It is widely believed that cancer is caused by a decline in the immune system caused by aging and other factors. The AIDS virus destroys immuno cells and triggers diseases.

Over time cell-mediated immunity may become inadequate or malfunction. This could allow multiple genetic mutations in the same location (malignant transformations) to reach cell proportions resulting in abnormal or malignant growth. The process is generally quite slow and it may take many years and many bouts of illness to truly manifest itself.

Therapists across the country have consistently observed the therapeutic benefits produced by Oriental mushrooms for a wide range of health problems. Oriental mushrooms have strong immune-stimulating properties, and can lead to improvement in the cases of common health problems ranging from cancer, chronic fatigue syndrome, high blood pressure, rheumatoid arthritis, diabetes, hepatitis, high cholesterol, constipation, cancer, tumors, HIV and AIDS.

To maintain good health, minimize the frequency and severity of all illnesses and recover quickly, and enjoy a healthy quality of life, it is imperative that the immune system is functioning efficiently and optimally. The more detriment we expose the body to, the harder the immune system has to work to maintain our health.

For all these reasons, natural immune system support is very important, making Agaricus blazei Murill an ideal food supplement for all of us.

Cancer - An Overview

Since much of the research on mushrooms and Agaricus blazei Murill involves its protective effects against cancer, it is important to review some of the basics on this serious killer.

While cancer is among the top two causes of death today, the most common types of cancer are largely *preventable.* Chemical and environmental factors may be responsible for 90% of all cancers. Exposure to these factors is greatly our own responsibility. Even hormone imbalances and toxic buildup in the cells, especially the colon, can be traced to the environment, such as our intake of pesticide and hormone residues. Additional cancer risk factors that are more difficult to control include genetics and age. The remaining factor is stress, which weakens our immune system.

Cancer is the abnormal growth of cells in our bodies. Cancer originates as a result of normal cell mutation through its genetic chromosome material, RNA and DNA.

Normally, cells replicate themselves continually at a rate synchronous with normal growth and repair in a manner specific for its purpose in the body. Cancerous cells multiply faster than normal and lose normal differentiation.

The actual mechanisms by which cancer is caused is still speculative. It involves a weakening and breakdown of the immune system. At any given time, there are literally thousands of potentially "precancerous" mutated cells throughout the body. A healthy immune system is able to effectively locate and eliminate them from the body. If it does not, the mutated cells turn cancerous.

We have all heard that cancer prevention is the best way to fight cancer. We are told not to smoke or drink and to avoid foods containing nitrates, pesticides and other chemicals, to avoid stress and even the sun (at least without sun-screen). These are all good suggestions, but the hidden message is that these things weaken our most important defense against cancer — the immune system. Maintaining a healthy intracellular environment helps prevent cancer, and correcting a toxic environment may lead to successful non-toxic treatment for cancer.

Mushroom extracts boost the immune system and combat viruses and bacteria, protect the body from cancer and may even shrink existing tumors.

Mushrooms For Immune Enhancement

Most studies on the health benefits of mushrooms for humans have focused on its immune enhancement properties. Mushroom polysaccharides (complex sugars) and their derivatives are able to stimulate cytokine production in humans. Cytokines are protein messenger molecules, which facilitate communication between cells to fight against pathogens. Cytokines mobilize the immune system and they also increase bone marrow production of other important immune system cells.

Complex cellular processes such as proliferation and differentiation are regulated in part by cytokines and other extracellular signaling molecules. Cytokines can exert their mitogenic effects by binding to specific cell surface receptor protein tyrosine kinases. This interaction triggers numerous biochemical responses, including changes in phospholipid metabolism, the activation of a protein phosphorylation cascade, and the enhanced expression of specific immediate-early, delayed-early, or late response genes. Some common cytokines include interleukins, interferon, natural killer cells (NK cells), activating factors and tumor necrosis factors (TNF).

Oriental mushrooms have been used as a tonic to increase energy, ward off hunger, extend longevity and promote overall vitality and virility. Historically, mushrooms have been recommended to reduce the frequency of colds and flu, kill intestinal worms, alleviate headaches, improve depressed libido, vision problems, constipation, hemorrhoids, stomach ache, diabetes, liver ailments, nerve pain, gout and other conditions.

Today, research indicates that mushroom extracts can boost the immune system and combat viruses and bacteria, protect the body from cancer and may even shrink existing tumors. Additional research suggests they may help:

- Lower blood cholesterol levels
- Balance blood pressure
- Inhibit platelet aggregation, thus reducing the likelihood of heart disease
- Assist in the treatment of AIDS, herpes, and other viral conditions
- Hepatitis and other liver conditions
- Chronic Fatigue Syndrome
- Influenza
- Tuberculosis
- Environmental allergies
- Bronchial inflammation
- Hodgkin's disease
- Stomach ulcers

Polysaccharides and Beta Glucan

While mushrooms contain several notable medicinal compounds, the most significant are the polysaccharides (high-molecular-weight complex sugars). These have attracted the most research interest. Polysaccharides, most notably beta glucan, have attracted research attention for their newly discovered immune-enhancing and/or tumor-retarding affects in the body. Oriental mushrooms have a very high content of beta-1.3 and 1.6-glucan, which researchers consider some of the most powerful. Of all Oriental mushrooms tested, the species Agaricus blazei Murill has the highest concentration of the polysaccharide, beta glucan.

When consumed orally, polysaccharides activate various immune effector cells (macrophages, natural killer cells, T-cells, etc.) to attack tumor cells, but also potentiate the activities of various immune mediators, including lymphokines, and interleuken-1 and interleuken-2. Lymphokines and interleuken-1 and -2 are important components of white blood cells that regulate the human immune system. Since Agaricus blazei Murill stimulates these cells, they exert a strong anti-tumor and regulatory effect upon the immune system.

Regulation of these immune cells is important not only to the possible prevention and treatment of cancer and tumors, but for other immune dysfunctions as well. For example, medicinal mushrooms produce anti-viral activities, and help regulate the immune system during chemotherapy and other highly stressful events.

In most cases, oral ingestion is more effective than direct injection. The polysaccharide complexes are partially broken down by the action of acids and enzymes in the digestive system, making them more readily available.

Beta Glucan

One of the most important of these phytochemical polysaccharides is beta glucan, also known as beta-D-glucan. The structure of immune-enhancing beta glucan is termed as beta (1,3) or (1,6) glucan. This means that glucose molecules are linked together in a so-called beta (1,3) chain, which forms the backbone of the beta-

Agaricus blazei Murrill contains the highest level of all the mushrooms tested for Beta Glucan!

glucan, with glucose molecules branching out from the backbone in beta (1,6) linkages.

Beta glucan is a unique compound derived from yeast. It is a non-digestible long-chain carbohydrate found in the cell walls of certain plants. Beta glucan may benefit an imbalanced immune system in several different ways. Beta glucan triggers an immune response in the body creating a system of defense against viral, bacterial, fungal, parasitic or potentially cancerous invaders. It is also a potent anti-oxidant free radical scavenger.

It is water soluble and effective when taken orally. There is no known toxicity or side effects from using beta glucan.

Beta glucan has been studied for more than 30 years as a supplement to improve immune function. The most important property of beta glucan is that it is an important immune activator. It increases nonspecific immunity and fosters resistance to infection. It does this by targeting and activating immune cells, primarily macrophages, but also other white blood cells including monocytes, neutrophils and precursor immune cells. Thus, macrophages, which means "big eaters," devour invading pathogens of all sorts.

Beta glucan benefits specific white blood cells of the immune system, especially macrophages. These white blood cell scavengers form a first line of defense against invaders and act as internal regulators of the immune system. When triggered by stimuli such as bacteria, viruses, endotoxins and toxic chemicals, macrophages can destroy dangerous cells and eliminate debris. Macrophages produce cytokines that activate and mobilize the immune system and also increase bone marrow production of immune cells. Beta glucan induces expression of cytokines which jump start the immune system in case of a precipitous threat.

Macrophage cell membranes possess specific receptors (or docking sites) for beta glucan. Upon binding of beta glucan to this receptor, the macrophages are activated to identify and eliminate invading pathogens from the body. Essentially, Beta glucan triggers a chain reaction leading to increased immune activity. As an example, Beta glucan steps up phagocytic activity by engulfing foreign cells, leading to the destruction of pathogens. It stimulates the production of interferon and interleukins to gear up defenses by activating T cells and other immune system cells. In addition, Beta glucan can trigger the release of tumor necrosis factor (TNF), a potent defensive protein and superoxide for human blood cells such as monocytes, to wage chemical warfare against invaders.

Reduced bone marrow proliferation implies lowered white cell counts and an increased risk of infection and cancer. Therefore, it is significant that beta glucan stimulates production of immune cells by the bone marrow. Other studies offer the prospect of protection against radiation damage: When mice were exposed to increasing levels of radiation, beta glucan administered pre- and post-irradiation decreased mortality. Stimulation of bone marrow cell production was a major benefit. In other studies, human natural killer cells, responsible for destroying cancer cells and other potentially harmful cells, were activated in the presence of beta glucan.

Immune Enhancing Effects of Beta Glucan:

- Increases production of cytokines
- Stimulates production of Interferon and other immune system enhancers
- Increases phagocytosis activity
- Activates natural killer cells
- Stimulates the production of inflammatory signal proteins such as interleukin-1
- Activates T cells and other immune system cells
- Triggers tumor necrosis factor (TNF) release

Medicinal mushrooms (containing beta glucan) have an ancient history of use as defensive allies in Japanese and Chinese medicine and folk traditions. Their immune-boosting benefits are derived from many different constituents, but complex (highly branched) beta glucan and their protein complexes are key features. For example, beta glucan such as grifolin from

Beta glucan activates macrophages to identify and eliminate invading pathogens from the body, triggering a chain reaction leading to increased immune activity.

maitake (Grifola frondosa) and lentinan from shiitake (Lentinus edodes) have been studied extensively for their immune enhancing and tumor-fighting properties.

Other Sources of Beta Glucan

In addition to Oriental mushrooms, beta glucan can also be isolated from the common bakers' yeast (Saccharomyces cerevisiae) algae, seaweed, oats, barley and aloe vera.

Oats are well known for the beta glucan they contain as a form of soluble dietary fiber, which forms a viscous gel. When consumed with a meal, oat beta glucan decreases the uptake of glucose (lowers the glycemic index of the food) and thus supports blood sugar regulation. Oat beta glucan can also decrease LDL cholesterol, the less desirable form of cholesterol, in individuals with high blood cholesterol levels.

There are also studies showing that beta glucans of mushroom origin (Pleurotus ostreatus) are able to help reduce serum levels of very-low-density lipoproteins (VLDL) and of LDL cholesterol (up to 40%) and decrease triglycerols by 27%. (Bobek)

History of Agaricus Blazei Murill

Agaricus blazei Murill (himematsutake) originates from Piedade, which is located in the suburbs of Sao Paulo, Brazil. The climactic conditions in Piedade include temperatures that soar to 35° C. during the day and dip to between 20-25° C. at night. The average humidity of 80%, due to daily squall, is the most ideal weather for ABM to grow in the wild. The quality and survival of Agaricus is significantly affected by these external conditions.

Natives for many years consumed it as part of their regular diet. In the mid 1960's, a researcher from Penn State noted that the rate of occurrence of adult diseases in the Piedade region was extremely low, and found that it was because the Agaricus mushroom was a part of the regular diet of the inhabitants of the Piedade region. A group of researchers, headed by Dr. W. J. Cinden of Pennsylvania State University and Dr. Lambert of Lambert Research Institute, went to the Piedade region. After months of rigorous study, they confirmed and reported that a regular diet of the type of mushroom contributes to their relative longevity.

At about the same time, Japan also noticed that the natives who regularly ate this type of mushroom seemed to possess a strong immune system that fought off various life threatening diseases.

Soon after this, Agaricus was introduced to Japan. Dr. Shoji Shibata, who at the time was a professor in the Pharmacological Department of Tokyo University, and

Agaricus Blazei Murill

Agaricus is often praised as the "Mushroom of God" or "The King of Mushrooms" due to it's health enhancing effects.

Dr. Tetuo Ikegawa of the National Cancer Center, jointly researched the pharmacological effects of Agaricus. The research results were released at the general convention of the Japan Pharmacological Association and the Japan Cancer Association in 1980. Their research with mice verified that the polysaccharide beta D glucan contained in Agaricus significantly activated the immune system.

Since that time, the popularity of Agaricus grew quickly as it became known as the health food that promotes a strong immune system and fights various life threatening illness including cancer.

In the last few years, some companies in China, Japan and the US have started cultivating Agaricus commercially in a hot house environment. There are some differences in the elements and ingredients due to variations in growing conditions.

Agaricus Blazei Murill Research

Agaricus blazei Murill is enjoying growing attention for its ability to enhance immunity. It does not only bolster immunity but reduces excessive immuno reactions to maintain a balance.

Of all fungi, Agaricus is particularly rich in beta

glucan polysaccharides, and has shown particularly strong results in treating and preventing cancer.

The table on the facing page shows the results of tests on the anti-cancer effects of Agaricus compared to other mushroom extracts conducted on guinea pigs at the Medical Department of Tokyo University, the National Cancer Center Laboratory and Tokyo College of Pharmacy. (Osaki)

Vaccinating a type of cancer cell (sarcoma 180) into guinea pigs normally causes cancer to spread to the entire body over four to five weeks, resulting in the death of almost all these animals. Agaricus extract was administered for 10 consecutive days. The results were then recorded four to five weeks later. The experiment was repeated on groups of between five and ten Guinea pigs, which were each given a different fungus extract. The mean values taken from these experiments were expressed as percentages.

The anti-cancer effect rate represents the percentage of guinea pigs which fully recovered from the cancer induced by an initial vaccination of sarcoma 180 and in whom a second vaccination of sarcoma 180 failed because the cancer cells could not be successfully embedded.

From these results, it was deduced that the Agaricus polysaccharide extract activates the immunity of normal biological tissue, so that even when a virus or other external factors enter the tissue, macrophage and interferon production within the tissue is vitalized to prevent the multiplication, metastasis and reoccurrence of cancer cells. Results of the experiments suggest that it also activates metabolism by revitalizing normal biological tissue.

MEDICAL DEPARTMENT OF TOKYO UNIVERSITY, THE NATIONAL CANCER CENTER LABORATORY AND TOKYO COLLEGE OF PHARMACY ANTI-CANCER RESULTS

Name of fungus	**Daily dosage**	**Rate of complete recovery**	**Anti-cancer effect**
Agaricus blazei Murill	10 mmg.	90.0%	99.4%
Grifola umbellate	10 mmg.	90.0%	98.5%
Phellinus yucatensis	30 mmg.	87.5%	96.5%
Phellinus igniarius	30 mmg.	66.7%	87.4%
Lenzites betulina	30 mmg.	57.1%	70.2%
Tricholoma matsutake	30 mmg.	55.5%	91.3%
Lentinus edodes	30 mmg.	54.5%	80.7%
Coriolus versicolor	30 mmg.	50.0%	77.5%
Pleurotus osteatus	30 mmg.	45.5%	75.3%
Elfringia applanata	30 mmg.	45.5%	64.9%
Fomitopsis pincicola	30 mmg.	33.3%	61.2%
Fomitopsis cytisna	30 mmg.	30.3%	44.2%
Pholiota nameko	30 mmg.	30.0%	86.5%
Flammulina velutipes	30 mmg.	30.0%	81.1%
Ganoderma Lucidum	30 mmg.	20.0%	77.8%

The table shows that Agaricus blazei Murill produced high results for both a complete recovery and for its anti-cancer effect. The experiment used guinea pigs of between five and six weeks old (equivalent to 15 and 16 human years). (Osaki)

Also note that a much lower dosage (10 mmg. vs. 30 mmg.) was required by the Agaricus compared to the other species, most likely due to the much higher beta glucan content in Agaricus. (Osaki)

Anti-Tumor Effects

Several research studies show that Agaricus blazei has anti-tumor activity in mammals. The polysaccharides contained in Agaricus vitalizes production of interferon and interleukin in small animals (guinea pigs). This effect indirectly functions to destroy or prevent the proliferation of cancer cells via a cytokine inducing effect.

Clinical results obtained in collaboration with university researchers and hospitals since the report on the anti-cancer effect of Agaricus was released at the general convention of the Japan Cancer Association in 1980, showed that many fungi polysaccharides only affect solid cancer. However, the polysaccharides of Agaricus are effective against Ehrlich's ascites carcinoma, sigmoid colonic cancer, ovarian cancer, breast cancer, lung cancer and liver cancer as well as against solid cancer.

Researchers have concluded that the results suggest that Oriental mushrooms would be effective enough to produce positive anti-tumor activity if administered to human cancer patients. Extensive clinical studies of Oriental mushrooms for colorectal and breast cancer patients are now underway.

Japanese researchers at the Department of Pharmacology, Mie University School of Medicine, examined the anti-tumor activity of the polysaccharide-protein complex prepared from Agaricus blazei against four kinds of established mouse tumors. (They called it ATOM, anti-tumor organic substance Mie.)

They found that it was highly effective against all four different types of tumors. They determined that the tumor growth-inhibitory effect is apparently due to immunological host-mediated mechanisms. The number of peritoneal macrophages increased and the level of phagocytosis activity increased in the mice treated with the polysaccharide complex. These results suggest that the macrophage activation and alterations of the C3 are necessary for the induction of an anti-tumor effect of the polysaccharide complex. (Ito)

Note: The Agaricus grade used in this study was of Silver grade. Brazilian Agaricus is usually rated a higher grade, Gold or Ultra Gold, meaning it would likely produce better results.

Another group of Japanese researchers at the Department of Agricultural Chemistry, Faculty of Agriculture, Shizuoka University, also determined that the polysaccharide-containing materials most active against tumors were comprised of protein and a 1,6-beta-D-glucan. (Kawagishi)

At Kobe University in Japan, researchers determined that Agaricus blazei polysaccharides stimulate lymphocyte T-cell subsets in mice. They found that white blood cells (T-cell, helper T-cells, cytotoxic T-cells,

> *"The broad spectrum of immunopharmacological activities of beta glucan includes not only the modification of certain bacterial, fungal, viral, and parasitic infection, but also inhibition of tumor growth."*
>
> Nicholas DiLuzio, Ph.D., Department of Physiology, Tulane University School of Medicine

CD4 and CD8) were significantly increased in mice orally administered Agaricus blazei polysaccharides. This activity was attributed to the polysaccharide complex of alpha-1,6- and alpha-1,4-glucan, which had already been shown to have anti-tumor activity against Sarcoma 180. The researchers commented that the Agaricus blazei polysaccharide may be an effective prophylactic, protecting humans against cancer by stimulating lymphocyte activity to eliminate potentially cancerous cells. (Mizuno)

This group of researchers also showed additional anti-tumor polysaccharides present in Agaricus. (Mizuno)

Researchers at the Korea Research Institute of Bioscience and Biotechnology, Taejon showed that polysaccharides from mushrooms stimulated humoral and cell mediated immunity. Overall, in vitro immune function was enhanced; stimulated immune functions of T lymphocytes, such as proliferation of T lymphocyte induced by mixed lymphocytes reaction and cytotoxicity of cytotoxic T-cells responding to alloantigen. Nonspecific immune functions mediated by natural killer cells and macrophages were increased by in vivo and in vitro treatment. (Kim)

Additional Antimutagenic and Bactericidal

Most of the cancer research on Agaricus has been done on the high level of Beta (1,3) D-glucan and Beta (1,6) D-glucan protein compounds it contains, however, this powerful immune-enhancing mushroom contains a number of additional tumor-fighting components! These include: ribonucleic acid protein compounds, acid heteroglucan, xyloglucan, lectin, etc. When these elements are introduced into our white blood cells, they enhance the activity of macrophage, an important antibody cell that destroys or delays the proliferation of tumor and cancer cells through phagocytosis.

Agaricus also contains natural steroids, known for their anti cancer effect. It is particularly effective in prevention of uterus cancer. Note: This is very different from the pharmaceutical chemically-produced steroids often said to be cancer causing.

Individuals from the Tokyo College of Pharmacy in Japan, isolated and identified the essential fatty acid linoleic acid as a main substance in Agaricus blazei having antimutagenic activity. A bactericidal, not antimutagenic, substance was also isolated and identified as 13-hydroxy cis-9, trans-11-octadecadienoic acid (13ZE-LOH). (Osaki)

Preventative effects:

Agaricus contains large amounts of non digestive dietary fibers that absorb cancerous materials in our body and discharge away from our system.

Agaricus can also be used as a complement to radiation or chemical therapy to prevent radiation damage and lessen the side effects.

Other Health Benefits

These are some of the major medicinal effects of Agaricus blazei Murill. It activates our own immune system to most naturally combat against dangerous organisms and bacteria.

Adaptogen Effects

Oriental mushrooms are adaptogens, which means they help the body to adapt to any form of physical or emotional stress, regulate endocrine functions and bring itself into balance (or homeostasis). Adaptogens can, for example, lower high blood pressure and raise low blood pressure. They have the same effect on blood sugar. Adaptogens regulate and normalize organs, glands and many other internal functions.

Oriental mushrooms may also be useful in the prevention and treatment of chronic hepatitis. In a research study, three human patients consuming 900 mg. of Oriental mushroom powder, 2-3 times daily for 40 days, manifested a significant improvement in liver enzymes (SGOT, SGPT and bilirubin) indicative of liver dysfunction.

Chronic Fatigue Syndrome

Oriental mushrooms may also prove beneficial in the prevention or treatment of Chronic Fatigue Syndrome (CFS). Patients with CFS have a deficient production of natural killer cell activity and abnormal T-lymphocyte levels. Research indicates that Oriental mushrooms can help balance these immune functions in patients. Adaptogenic herbs and Oriental mushrooms may prove quite beneficial in the prevention and treatment of chronic immune degenerative disorders.

Immune Deficiency

Laboratory studies conducted at the U.S. National Cancer Institute, and the Japanese National Institutes of Health, showed that Oriental mushroom extracts kill the Human Immunodeficiency Virus (HIV) and enhance the activity of T-helper cells. T-helper cells are important components of the human immune system that kill harmful cells in the body, such as HIV and cancer.

A preliminary study of 10 AIDS patients indicated that 8 grams per day of Oriental mushroom powder for three months increased T-helper cell count, while improving typical AIDS symptoms, such as dry cough, dermatitis and insomnia.

Individuals with severely depleted immune systems are highly sensitive and reactive to many substances. Dried Oriental mushroom products are a safe, non-toxic therapy, and help accelerate the rate of self-healing when used in treatment of many immune-related health problems and other disorders.

Auto-Immune Conditions

Researchers have also observed improvement in individuals using Agaricus blazei Murill and other mushrooms in individuals with various autoimmune conditions such as rheumatoid arthritis, diabetes, Lupus, atopic dermatitis and others. (Higaki)

Alopecia areata (complete loss of hair) is believed to be an autoimmune condition often triggered by stress. Stress (even such as chemotherapy) can greatly increase the work load of the immune system. Stress can also increase hair loss without causing Alopecia. (Gupta)

Melanin, a protein effective in the production of hair, is present in Agaricus. Melanin is also found in semen and egg whites. Melanin incontinence or clumping is associated with Alopecia areata. (Gardner) It would be interesting to see if Agaricus supplementation, due to its immune enhancing effects and melanin content, would have a beneficial effect on hair loss associated with stress. I could not locate published studies on this subject.

Diabetes

Preliminary research and direct therapeutic observation indicates that Agaricus may be helpful in lowering blood glucose levels and preventing or treating diabetes. The Beta (1,3) D-glucan and Beta (1,6) D-glucan protein compounds, ribonucleic acid protein compounds help reduce elevated blood glucose.

A study conducted at the Institute of Longevity Medicine showed that blood sugar was significantly lowered (11.1%) after seven days administration of 8% Agaricus powder. (See)

A study showed that feeding Agaricus powder to diabetic rats lowered their blood glucose levels from 450 mg./dl to 150 mg./dl. No reduction in blood glucose was seen in the control animals. Therapists confirm that Oriental mushrooms may prove beneficial for diabetics. (See, Higaki)

Supports Healthy Bones!

Argaricus contains Vitamin B1 and B2 but also contains large amounts of ergosterol, which would be converted to Vitamin D2 when it is dried in the sun or heated in a mechanical drying process. Vitamin D2 has positive effects to lessen the danger of bone loss.

Blood Pressure, Cholesterol, Arteriosclerosis

Agaricus contains digestive dietary fibers (such as beta glucan) and unsaturated fatty acids, such as linolin, have effects to reduce blood pressure, cholesterol and arteriosclerosis. Some of the beneficial effects are also attributed to tyrosinase, an enzyme which oxidizes tyrosine and produces melanin, which has a hypotensive effect.

Digestion

Digestive enzymes such as amylase trypsin martase and the protease contained in Agaricus blazei Murill and other mushrooms also enhance digestion.

Skin Problems/Wound Healing

The topical benefits of Agaricus benefits include skin rejuvenation, prevention and treatment of UV-related skin damage and wound healing. Additionally, beta-1,3-D-glucan may be injected into certain types of skin tumors. However, this use while shown to be effective almost 20 years ago - has not been widely utilized.

The beta glucan content and other agents that speed healing in Agaricus blazei Murill make it excellent to help heal rashes, blemishes, damaged skin and other such imperfections.

Some beta glucan products are available which are designed to reduce the signs of aging. Wrinkles are essentially the result of damage to the collagen tissues under the skin surface. Beta glucan may help by encouraging resurfacing by speeding skin cell renewal.

> *"For almost 10 years I had atopic dermatitis all over my body. It was like an allergic rash. I tried several things and nothing helped. I started drinking a tea made with about 2 grams of Agaricus blazei Murill every day. It took about 6 months, but by then, it was completely gone and has not returned in over a year and a half. I know by this, it supports the immune system." M.I.*

Agaricus Nutritional Data

The fresh fruitbody of Agaricus blazei Murill contains 85-87% water. Their mycelium contain 40-45% protein, 38-45% polysaccharides, 6-8% cellulose, 5-7% ash and 3-4% fat.

Dried, the water content is less than 5%. Other constituents are approximately 40% protein, 38.4% polysaccharides, 8% cellulose, 7% ash and 3.8% fat.

The mineral content per 100 grams is as follows: Potassium (K) 26 mg., Phosphorous (P) 10 mg., Zinc (Zn) 5 mg., Cuprum (Cu) 4 mg., Plumbum (Pb) 3 mg. In smaller amounts are: Scadium (Sc), Calcium (Ca), Magnesium (Mg), Iron (Fe), Manganese (Mn), and Hydrargyrum (Hg).

Using Agaricus Blazei Murill

Agaricus blazei Murill is used as a tea, in capsules or even eaten fresh or dried, The minimum daily consumption of Agaricus should be about 5 or 6 grams.

However, the amount can be adjusted according to one's own health condition. For example, for cancer patients, the recommend daily dosage is approximately 40 grams. Therapeutic dosages can also be safely used in individuals with AIDS, or other life threatening situations. Regular dosages can be used for individuals with high cholesterol, high blood pressure, etc.

Agaricus has no known side effects. It has shown to be very safe in toxicity studies. (See)

Tea Preparation

Place approximately 15 - 20 grams (should last one person about three days) of dried Agaricus blazei Murill in about two liters of cold water for about 2 - 3 hours. Using a ceramic or hot glass pot, bring to boil and simmer at a low heat until the extract evaporates to about two-thirds of it's original volume. Remove the mushroom and after cooling off, keep it refrigerated and consume hot or cold over the next few days. Removed mushrooms still can be consumed in any recipe you want to add mushrooms to.

Drink a cup of Agaricus tea in the morning and evening. If you do not like the mushroom taste of the tea, you can add juice or milk to camouflage the taste.

Topical Use

Agaricus blazei Murill containing lotions and creams are available. You can also apply Agaricus directly by adding about 1/2 gram to about 3 tablespoons of boiling water. Apply directly to face or affected area with cotton twice daily. Store remainder in small glass container in the refrigerator for about three days.

Storage

Dried Agaricus should be kept in an air tight container such as plastic ware with sealable lids preferably with desiccant agent. For long term storage, the air tight container should be refrigerated.

Look for Quality Agaricus Blazei Murill

Many different grades of Agaricus are now available from Brazil, China, Japan and Korea. The best, containing the highest level of polysaccharides is graded Extra-

Gold, medium is Gold, and the lowest is Silver. The lower the grade the lower the amounts of polysaccharides they contain, and the less effective they are.

The variances in quality are based on growing and processing conditions of the mushrooms. The climate is a major factor. Brazillian Agaricus is usually graded Gold or Ultra Gold, Chinese and Japanese Agaricus is usually graded Silver due to climactic conditions.

Other factors include whether they are organically or chemically fertilized, and whether they are raised in natural sunlight or a green house environment. Carelessness by some producers may result in over drying and burning of the mushrooms resulting in lower grades. Freeze drying drastically reduces and destroys the polysaccharides. Only careful natural drying preserves the best quality.

Agaricus planted in nature, and raised in nature, using natural biological compost from animals living in a natural organic environment, tend to produce higher polysaccharides levels than Agaricus grown in green houses or caves. Look for beta glucan yields of at least 4.8 grams per liter.

Other Immune-enhancing Mushrooms

Reishi. Anti-tumor, antibacterial, antioxidant, cardiotonic, immunopotentiation, enhanced NK cell activity, anti-HIV, antihistiminic, increased interleuki production, liver protecting and detoxifying, lowers cholesterol, protects against radiation, protects against altitude sickness, calming and relaxing, expectorant, antitussive.

Maitake. Anti-tumor, protects the liver, lowers blood pressure, stimulates T-cells, lowers blood sugar.

Shiitake. Anti-tumor, immunostimulating, immunoregulatory, antiviral, protects the liver, lowers cholesterol, lowers blood pressure, soothes bronchial inflammation, regulates urinary incontinence.

Hericium. Aids digestion, promotes strength and vigor, inhibits cancer.

Cordyceps. Effective for aging disorders such as loss of sex drive, lowers cholesterol, relaxes smooth muscle tissue in asthma, immunostimulating, antiarrhythmic, stops tinnitus when caused by inner ear fluid, improves liver function and is hepatoprotective.

Coriolus. Immunostimulating, antiviral, anti-HIV, anti-tumor, antioxidant, antibiotic.

Polyporus. Immunostimulating, anti-tumor (especially lung cancer and leukemia) diuretic.

Wood ear. Immunostimulating, lowers cholesterol and triglycerides.

Poria. Anti-tumor, antimutagenic.

Tremella. Immunostimulating, cardiotonic, lowers cholesterol, anti-inflammatory, lowers blood sugar, protects the liver, antiaging by increasing SOD and inhibiting MAO B.

Maintain Optimal Immunity

- Do not allow yourself to be overcome with stress.
- Avoid fatigue and get enough sleep.
- Do not smoke or drink excessively.
- Eat organic foods and drink pure (distilled is best) water whenever possible.
- Avoid processed foods, sugar, caffeine and other non-nutritives.
- Avoid exposure to toxins and chemicals.
- Maintain a balanced diet with optimal intake of fresh fruits and vegetables.
- Exercise regularly and moderately.
- Supplement antioxidants to ward off free radical damage.

While many lifestyle choices can negatively impact the health of your immune system, nutrition forms a foundation for keeping this defense strong and vigilant. Specific phytochemicals, especially beta glucan in Agaricus blazei Murill, may help to activate specific types of immune cells, to gear up defenses against potentially harmful microorganisms and to rebalance overactive immune defenses.

Bibliography

Adachi Y, Ohno N, Yadmae T; Activation of murine kupffer cells by administration with gel-forming (1-3)-beta-D-glucan from Grifola frondosa. Biol Pharm Bull 1998;21(3)278-83.

Babineau TJ, Hackford A, Kenler A, et al; A phase II multiple center, double-blind, randomized, placebo-controlled study of three dosages of an immunomodulator (PGG-glucan) in high risk surgical patients. Arch Surg 1994;129(11):1204-10.

Behall KM, Scholfield DJ, Hallfrisch J; Effect of Beta glucan level in oat fiber extracts on blood lipids in men and women. J Am Coll Nutr 1997;16(1)46-51.

Bobek P; Galbavy S; The oyster mushroom (Pleurotus ostreatus) effectively prevents the development of atherosclerosis in rabbits] Vyskumny ustav vyzivy, Bratislava. Ceska Slov Farm 1999 Sep;48(5):226-30

Bobek P; Galbavy S; Hypocholesterolemic and antiatherogenic effect of oyster mushroom (Pleurotus ostreatus) in rabbits. Research Institute of Nutrition, Bratislava, Slovak Republic.Nahrung 1999 Oct;43(5):339-42

Bobek P; Ozdin O; Mikus M; Dietary oyster mushroom (Pleurotus ostreatus) accelerates plasma cholesterol turnover in hypercholesterolaemic rat. Physiol Res 1995;44(5):287-91.

Chang, R; Functional properties of edible mushrooms, Nutr Rev (1996), 54(11 Pt 2):S91-93.

Chihara G; Recent progress in immunopharmacology and therapeutic effects of polysaccharides. Dev Biol Stand 1992;77:191-7.

Ebina T, Fujimiya Y; Antitumor effect of a peptide-glucan preparation extracted from Agaricus blazei in a double-grafted tumor system in mice. Division of Immunology, Miyagi Cancer Center Research Institute, Natori, Miyagi, Japan. Biotherapy 1998;11(4):259-65.

Di Renzo L, Yefenof E, Klien E; The function of human NK cells is enhanced by beta glucan, a ligand of CR3 (CD11b/CS18). Eur J Immunol 1991;21(7)1755-8.

Fujimiya Y, Suzuki Y, Oshiman K, Kobori H, Moriguchi K, Nakashima H, Matumoto Y, Takahara S, Ebina T, Katakura R; Selective tumoricidal effect of soluble proteoglucan extracted from the basidiomycete, Agaricus blazei Murill, mediated via natural killer cell activation and apoptosis. Division of Immunology, Miyagi Cancer Center Research Institute, Natori, Japan. Cancer Immunol Immunother 1998 May;46(3):147-59.

Fujimiya Y,Suzuki Y, Katakura R, Ebina T; Tumor-specific cytocidal and immunopotentiating effects of relatively low molecular weight products derived from the basidiomycete, Agaricus blazei Murill. Division of Immunology, Miyagi Cancer Center Research Institute, Natori, Japan. Anticancer Res 1999 Jan-Feb;19(1A):113-8.

Gardner S, Freyschmidt-Paul P, Hoffmann R, Sundberg JP, Happle R, Lindsey NJ, Tobin DJ; Normalisation of hair follicle morphology in C3H/HeJ alopecia areata mice after treatment with squaric acid dibutylester. University of Bradford, Bradford, West Yorkshire, England. Eur J Dermatol 2000 Aug;10(6):443-50.

Gupta MA, Gupta AK, Watteel GN; Stress and alopecia areata: a psychodermatologic study. Department of Psychiatry, University of Western Ontario, London,

Canada.Acta Derm Venereol 1997 Jul;77(4):296-8.

Hamuro J, Rollinghoff M, Wagner H; beta (1 leads to 3) Glucan-mediated augmentation of alloreactive murine cytotoxic T lymphocytes in vivo. Cancer Res 1978;38(9):3080-5.

Higaki M; Eguchi F; Watanabe Y; A stable culturing method and pharmacological effects of the Agaricus blazei] Lab. of Forest Products Chemistry, Tokyo University of Agriculture, Japan. Nippon Yakurigaku Zasshi 1997 Oct;110 Suppl 1:98P-103P.

Hofer M, Pospisil M. Glucan as a stimulator of hematopoeisis in normal and gamma-irradiated mice. Int J Immunopharmacol 1997;19(19)607-9.

Ito H, Shimura K, Itoh H, Kawade M; Antitumor effects of a new polysaccharide-protein complex (ATOM) prepared from Agaricus blazei (Iwade strain 101) "Himematsutake" and its mechanisms in tumor-bearing mice. Department of Pharmacology, Mie University School of Medicine, Japan. Anticancer Res 1997 Jan-Feb;17(1A):277-84.

Itoh H, Ito H, Amano H, Noda H; Inhibitory action of a beta-D-glucan-protein complex (F III-2-b) isolated from Agaricus blazei Murill ("himematsutake") on Meth A fibrosarcoma-bearing mice and its antitumor mechanism. Mie University, Japan. Jpn J Pharmacol 1994 Oct;66(2):265-71.

Kawagishi H, Inagaki R, Kanao T, Mizuno T, Shimura K, Ito H, Hagiwara T, Nakamura T; Fractionation and antitumor activity of the water-insoluble residue of Agaricus blazei fruiting bodies. Department of Agricultural Chemistry, Faculty of Agriculture, Shizuoka University, Japan. Carbohydr Res 1989 Mar 15;186(2):267-73

Kim HM, Han SB, Oh GT, Kim YH, et al; Stimulation of humoral and cell mediated immunity by polysaccharide from mushroom Phellinus linteus. Korea Research Institute of Bioscience and Biotechnology, Taejon. Int J Immunopharmacol 1996 May;18(5):295-303.

Kulicke WM, Lettau AI, Thielking H; Correlation between immunological activity, molecular mass and molecular structure of different (1-3)-beta-D-glucan. Carbohydr Res 1997;297(2)135-42.

Liang J, Melican D, Cafro L et al; Enhanced clearance of a multiple antibiotic resistant Staphylococcus aureus in rats treated with PBB-glucan is associated with increased leukocyte counts and increased neutrophil oxidative burst activity. Int J Immunopharmacol 1998;20(11)595-614.

Mizuno M, Minato K, Ito H, Kawade M, Terai H, Tsuchida H; Anti-tumor polysaccharide from the mycelium of liquid-cultured Agaricus blazei mill. Graduate School of Science and Technology, Kobe University, Japan. Biochem Mol Biol Int 1999 Apr;47(4):707-14.

Mizuno M, Morimoto M, Minato K, Tsuchida H; Polysaccharides from Agaricus blazei stimulate lymphocyte T-cell subsets in mice. Division of Science of Biological Resources, Graduate School of Science and Technology, Kobe University, Japan. Biosci Biotechnol Biochem 1998 Mar;62(3):434-7.

Ohno N, Asada N, Adachi Y et al; Enhancement of LPS triggered TNF-alpha (tumor necrosis factor-alpha) production by (1-3) beta-D-glucan in mice. Biol Pharm Bull 1995;8(1):126-33.

Osaki Y, Kato T, Yamamoto K, Okubo J, Miyazaki T; Antimutagenic and bactericidal substances in the fruit body of a Basidiomycete Agaricus blazei, Jun-17] Tokyo College of Pharmacy, Japan. Yakugaku Zasshi 1994 May;114(5):342-50.

Patchen ML, Liang J, Vaudrain T, et al; Mobilization of peripheral progenitor cells by Betafectin PGG-glucan alone and in combination with granulocyte colony-stimulating factor. Stem Cells 1998;16(3)208-17.

Penna C, Dean PA, Nelson H; Pulmonary metastases neutralization and tumor rejection by in vivo administration of Beta glucan and bispecific antibody. Int J Cancer 1996; 65(3)377-82.

Tamuro J, Rollinghoff M, Wagner H; beta (1 leads to 3) Glucan-mediated augmentation of alloreactive murine cytotoxic T lymphocytes in vivo. Cancer Res 1978;38(9):3080-5.

Thornton BP, Vetvicka V, Pitman M, et al; Analysis of the sugar specificity and molecular location of the Beta glucan binding lectin site of complement receptor type 3. J Immunol 1996;156(3):1235-46.

Tsujinaka T, Yokota M, Kambayashi J, et al; Modification of septic processes by Beta glucan administration. Eur Surg Res 1990;22(6):340-6.

Tzianabos AO, Gibson FC 3rd, Cisneros RL, Kasper DL.; Protection against experimental intra-abdominal sepsis by two polysaccharide immunomodulators. J Infect Dis 1998;178(1)200-6.

Sakurai T, Hashimoto K, Suzuki I, et al; Enhancement of murine alveolar macrophage functions by orally administered beta glucan. Int J Immunopharmacol 1992;14(5)821-30.

See, D, Agaricus blazei Murill Testing, Institute of Longevity Medicine, Huntington Beach, CA . 1999: Oct 27.

INDEX

ABOUT THE AUTHOR

Beth M. Ley, Ph.D., has been a science writer specializing in health and nutrition for over 12 years and has written over a dozen health related books, including the best sellers, ***DHEA: Unlocking the Secrets to the Fountain of Youth*** and ***MSM: On Our Way Back to Health With Sulfur***. She wrote her own undergraduate degree program and graduated in Scientific and Technical Writing from North Dakota State University in 1987 (combination of Zoology and Journalism). Beth has her masters (1997) and doctoral degrees (1999) in Nutrition.

Beth lives in the Minnesota lakes country. She is dedicated to God and to spreading the health message. She enjoys spending time with her Dalmatian, exercises on a regular basis, eats a vegetarian, low-fat diet and takes anti-aging supplements.

Memberships: American Nutraceutical Association, American Academy of Anti-aging, New York Academy of Sciences, Oxygen Society.

ORDER THESE GREAT BOOKS
FROM BL PUBLICATIONS!

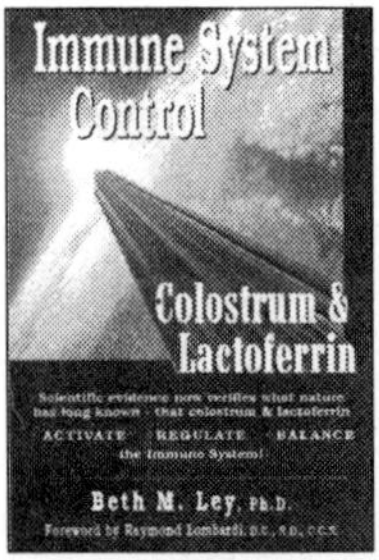

Immune System Control
Colostrum & Lactoferrin
Beth M. Ley, Ph.D. 200 pages, $12.95 ISBN 1-890766-11-9
Get the indepth and detailed FACTS about colostum and lactoferrin! Testimonials and much more! Also features a special product selection guide! Fully referenced/Indexed

Fading: One family's journey with a woman silenced by Alzheimer's - also with Preventative, Nutritional and Psychological Help for the Families and Patients with Alzheimer's Disease
Frances Kraft, Dr. Barry Kraft, Dr. Beth Ley, 2000, 200 pgs. $12.95
An excellent inspirational and resource book for all families and caretakers.

Aspirin Alternatives:
The Top Natural Pain-Relieving Analgesics
Raymond Lombardi, D.C., N.D., C.C.N., 1999, 160 pages, $8.95
This book discusses analgesics and natural approaches to pain. Ibuprofen and acetaminophen are used for pain-relief, but like all drugs, there is a risk of side effects and interactions, There are a number of natural alternatives which are equally effective and in many cases may be preferable because they may help treat the underlining problem rather than simply treating a symptom.

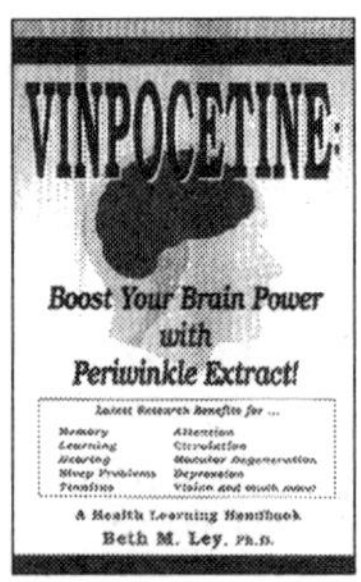

Vinpocetine: Boost Your Brain w/ Periwinkle Extract! Beth M. Ley, Ph.D. 2000, 48 pgs. $4.95
This herbal extract benefits: Memory, attention and concentration, learning, circulation, hearing, insomnia, depression, tinnitus, vision & more! Vinpocetine increases circulation in the brain and increases metabolism in the brain by increasing use of glucose and oxygen. Benefits both the old and young!

Coenzyme Q10: All Around Nutrient for All-Around Health!
Beth M. Ley-Jacobs, Ph.D., 1999, 60 pages, $4.95
CoQ10 is found in every living cell. With age, insufficient levels become more common, putting us at serious risk of illness and disease. Protect and strengthen the cardiovascular system; benefit blood pressure, immunity, fatigue, weight problems, Alzheimer's, Parkinson's, Huntington's, gum-disease and slow aging.

MSM: On Our Way Back To Health With Sulfur Beth M. Ley, 1998, 40 pages, $3.95

MSM (methyl sulfonyl methane), is a rich source of organic sulfur, important for connective tissue regeneration. Beneficial for arthritis and other joint problems, allergies, asthma, skin problems, TMJ, periodontal conditions, pain relief, and much more! Includes important "How to use" directions.

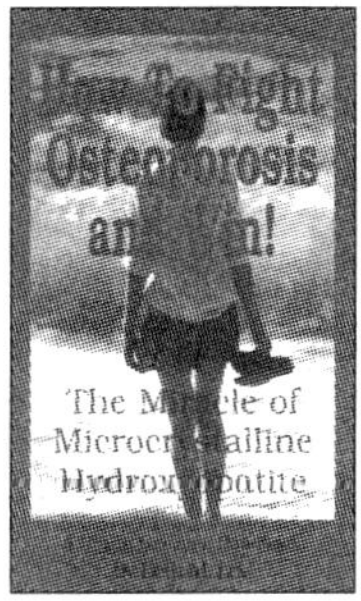

How to Fight Osteoporosis & Win: The Miracle of MCHC
Beth M. Ley, 80 pgs. $6.95

Find out if you are at risk for osteroporosis and what to do to prevent and reverse it. Get the truth about bone loss, calcium, supplements, foods, MCHC & much more! Find out what supplements can help you most!

Nature's Road to Recovery: Nutritional Supplements for The Social Drinker, Alcoholic & Chemical-Dependent
Beth M. Ley-Jacobs, Ph.D., 1999, 72 pages, $5.95

Recovery involves much more than abstinence. Cravings, depression, memory loss, liver problems, vascular problems, sexual problems, sleep problems, nutritional deficiencies and common health problems which can benefit from 5-HTP, DHA, phospholipids, St. John's Wort, antioxidants, etc.

DHA: The Magnificent Marine Oil
Beth M. Ley-Jacobs, Ph.D., 1999, 120 pages, $6.95

Individuals commonly lack this essential Omega-3 fatty acid so important to the brain, vision, and immune system and much more. Memory, depression, ADD, addiction disorders (especially alcoholism), inflammatory disorders, skin problems, schizophrenia, elevated blood lipids, etc., benefit from DHA.

Marvelous Memory Boosters Beth M. Ley, Ph.D. 2000, 32 pages, $3.95

Certain nutrients & phytochemicals (Alpha GPC, Vinpocetine, Huperzine-A, Pregnenolone, Phospholipids, DHA, Bacopa Monniera, Ginkgo Biloba, etc.) improve short & long term memory, increase mental acuity & concentration, improve learning abilities & mental stamina, reduce fatigue, improve sleep, mood, vision & hearing.

TO PLACE AN ORDER:

of copies

___ *Aspirin Alternatives: The Top Natural Pain-Relieving Analgesics* (Lombardi) $8.95

___ *Bilberry & Lutein: The Vision Enhancers!* (Ley) $4.95

___ *Calcium Facts: Fossilized Coral* (Ley) $4.95

___ *Castor Oil: Its Healing Properties* (Ley) $3.95

___ *Dr. John Willard on Catalyst Altered Water* (Ley) $3.95

___ *Co Q10: All-Around Nutrient for All-Around Health* (Ley) . $4.95

___ *Colostrum: Nature's Gift to the Immune System* (Ley) $5.95

___ *DHA: The Magnificent Marine Oil* (Ley Jacobs) $6.95

___ *DHEA: Unlocking the Secrets of the Fountain of Youth- 2nd Edition* (Ash-Ley) $14.95

___ *Discover the Beta Glucan Secret* (Ley) $3.95

___ *Fading: One family's journey with a women silenced by Alzheimer's (Kraft)* $12.95

___ *God Wants You Well* (Ley) $14.95

___ *Health Benefits of Probiotics* (Dash) $4.95

___ *How to Fight Osteoporosis and Win!* (Ley) $6.95

___ *Immune System Control-Colostrum & Lactoferrin* (Ley) $12.95

___ *Marvelous Memory Boosters* (Ley) $3.95

___ *Medicinal Mushrooms: Agaricus Blazei Murill (Ley)* $4.95

___ *MSM: On Our Way Back to Health W/ Sulfur* (Ley) $3.95

___ *Natural Healing Handbook* (Ley) $14.95

___ *Nature's Road to Recovery: Nutritional Supplements for the Alcoholic & Chemical Dependent* (Ley Jacobs) $5.95

___ *PhytoNutrients: Medicinal Nutrients Found in Foods* (Ley) $3.95

___ *The Potato Antioxidant: Alpha Lipoic Acid* (Ley) $6.95

___ *Vinpocetine: Revitalize Your Brain w/ Periwinkle Extract!* (Ley) $4.95

___ *Yesterday, Today & Tomarrow: Take the High Road to Health with Rod Burreson* (Burreson) $24.95

Book subtotal $ ____________ Please add $3.00 for shipping

TOTAL $____________

Send check or money order to:

BL Publications 14325 Barnes Drive Detroit Lakes, MN 56501

Credit card orders call toll free: 1-877-BOOKS11

also please visit www.blpbooks.com